This Belongs To:

____

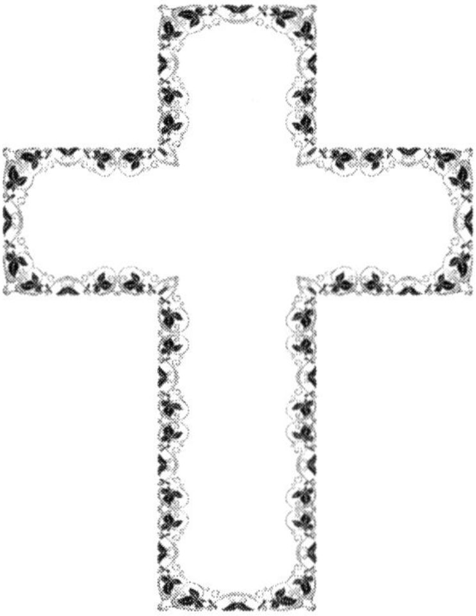

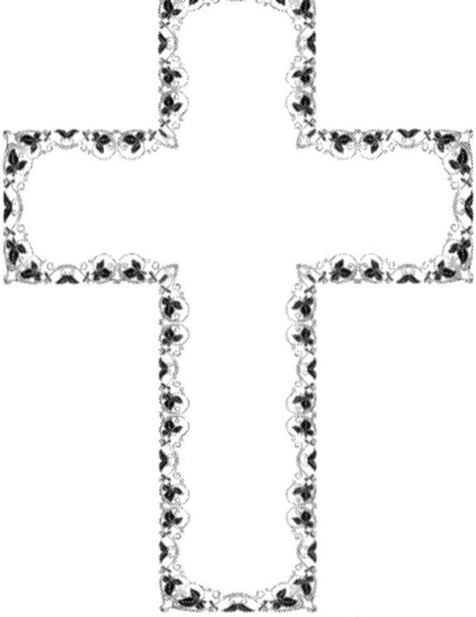

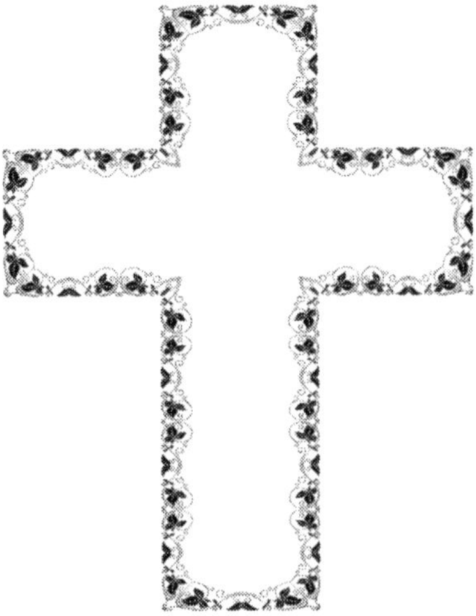

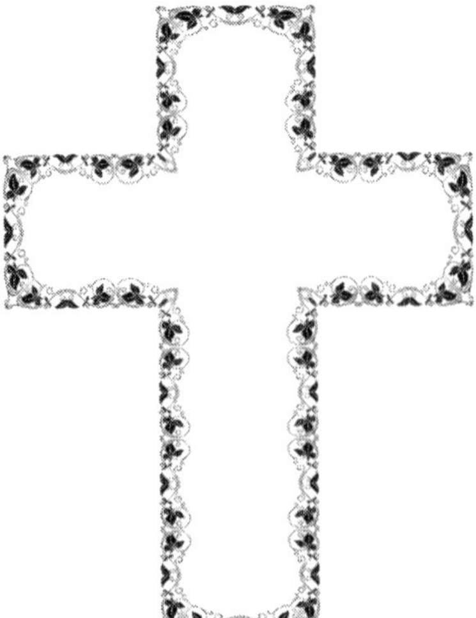

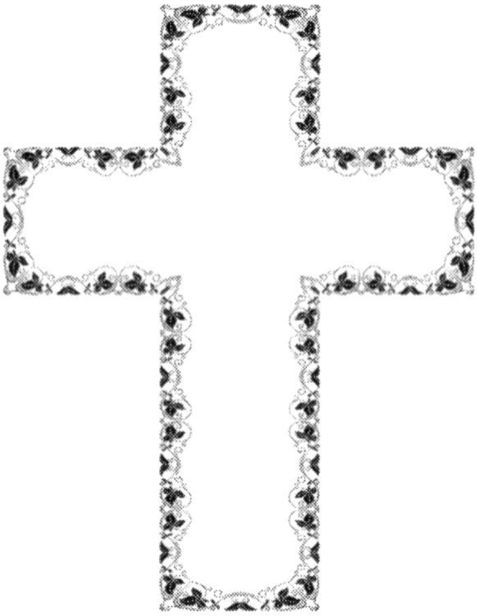

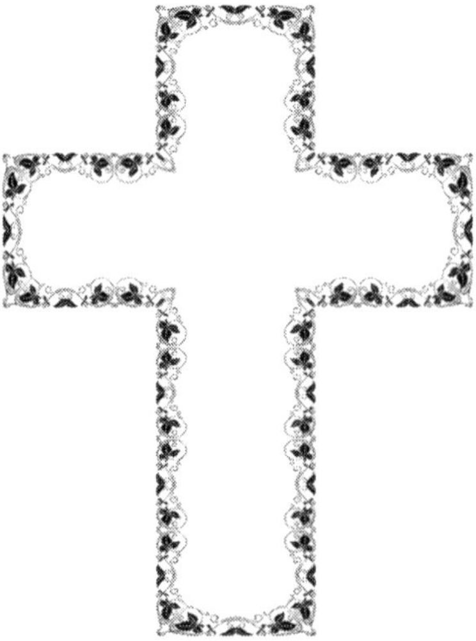

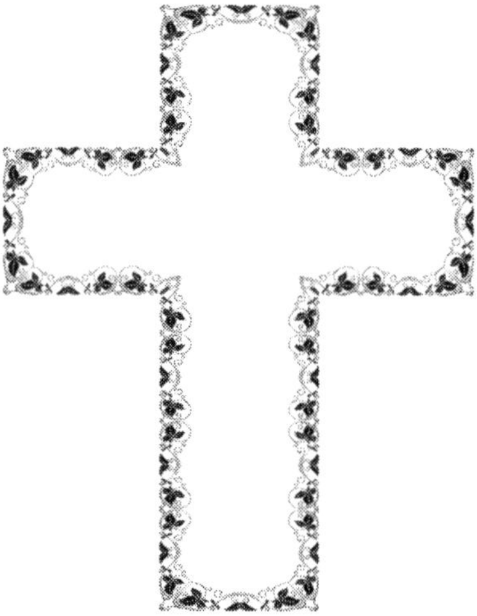

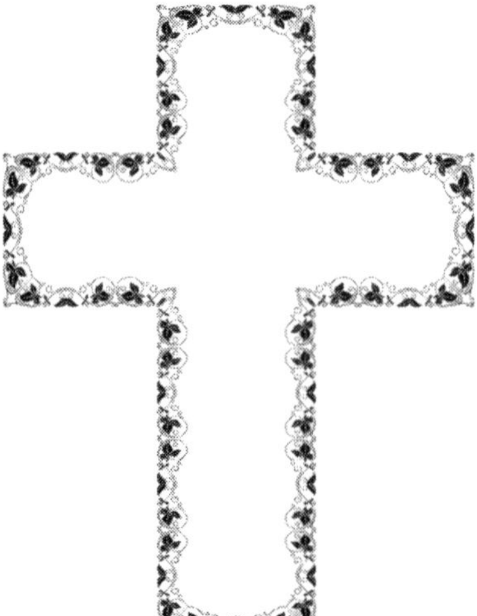

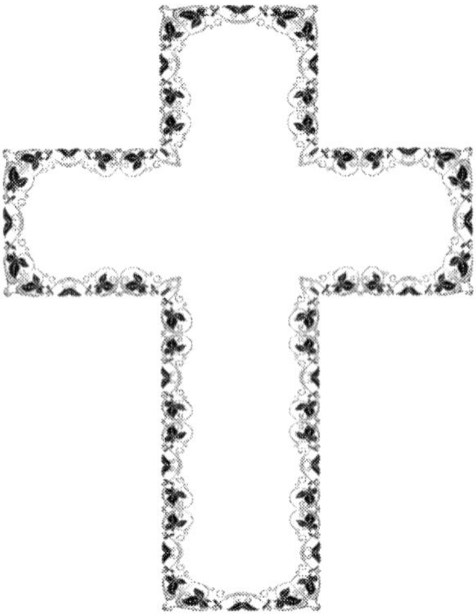

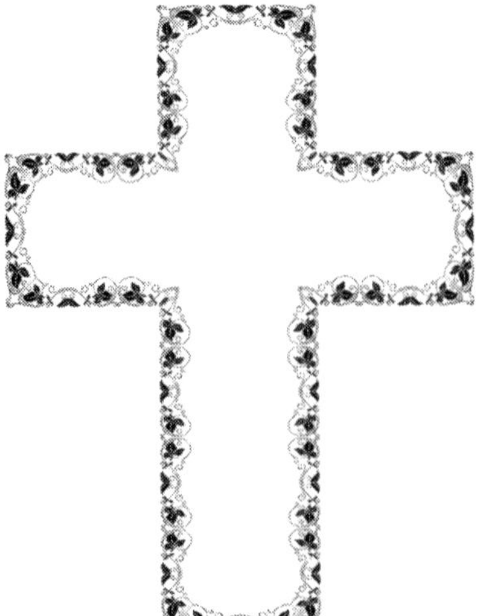

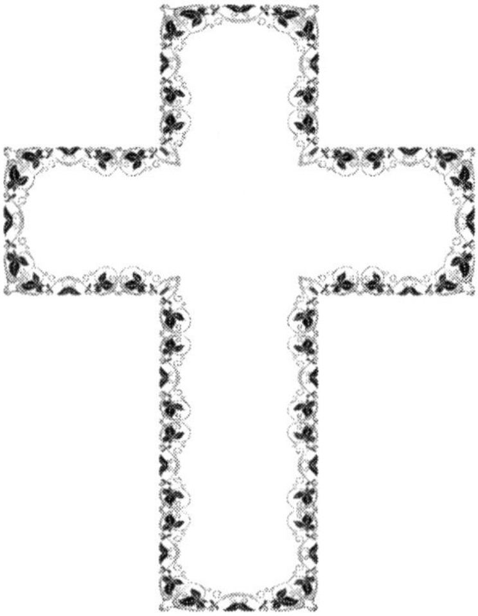

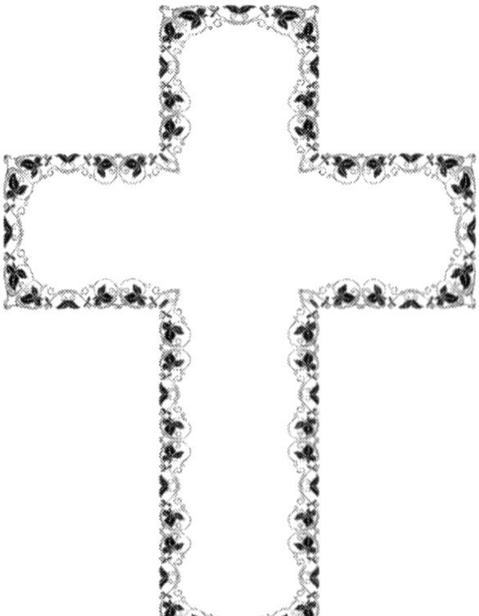

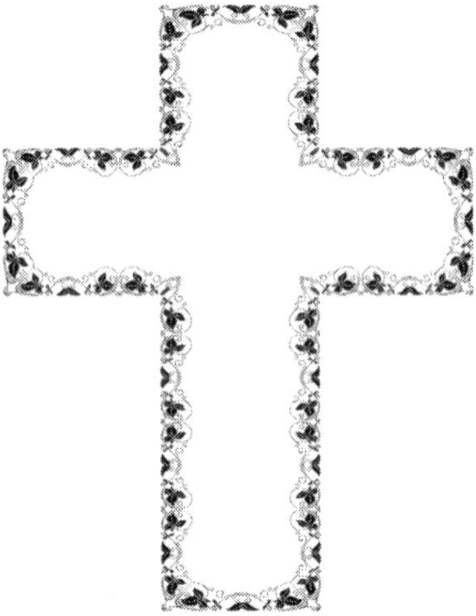

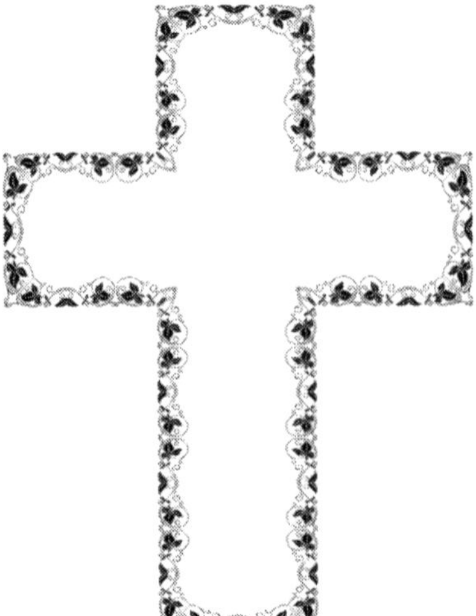

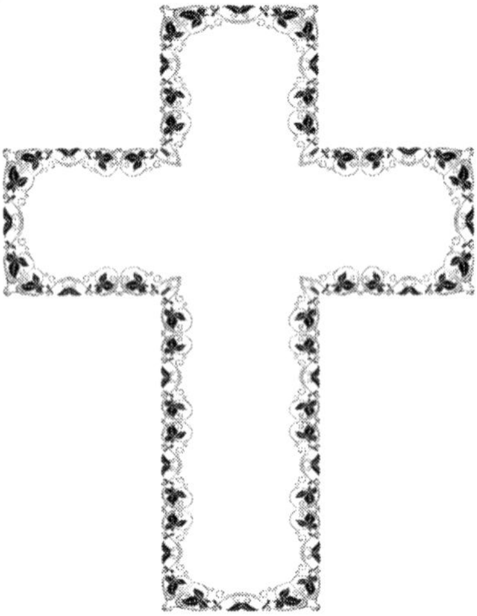

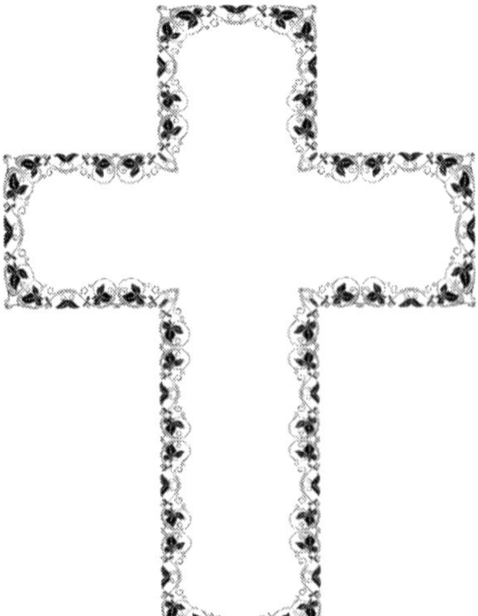

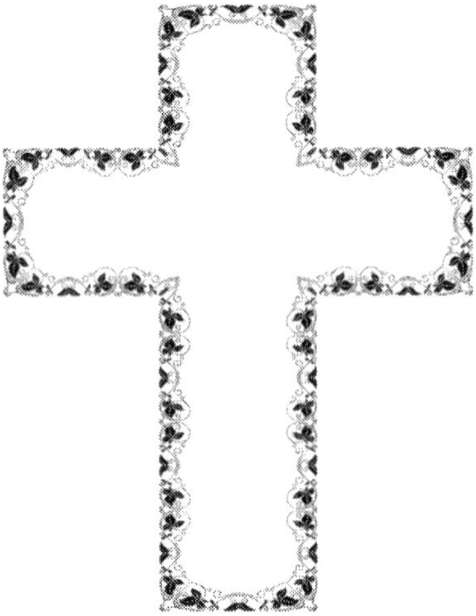

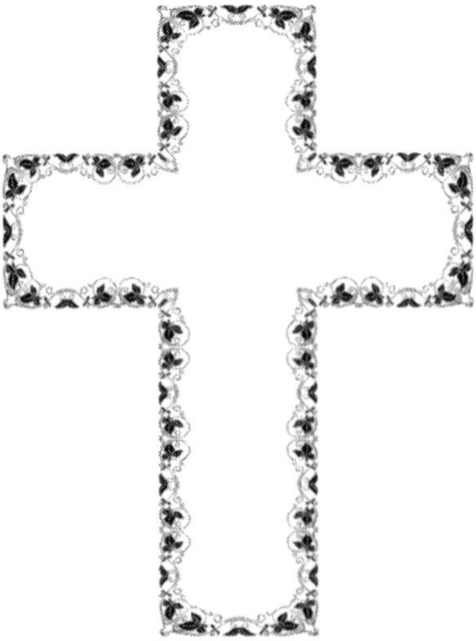

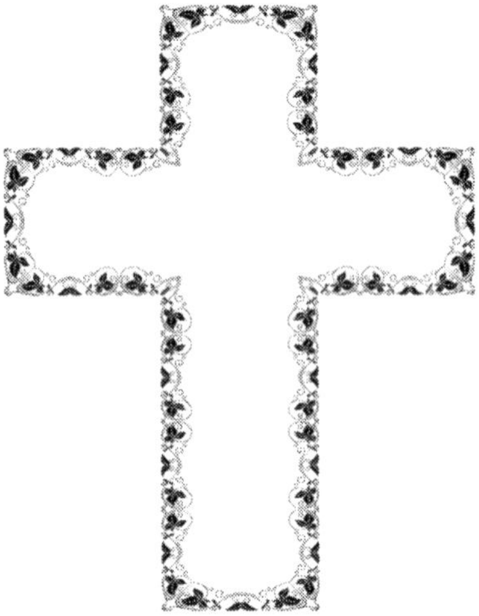

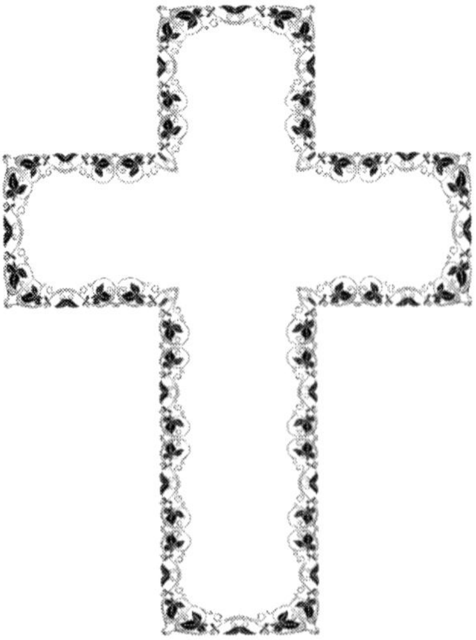

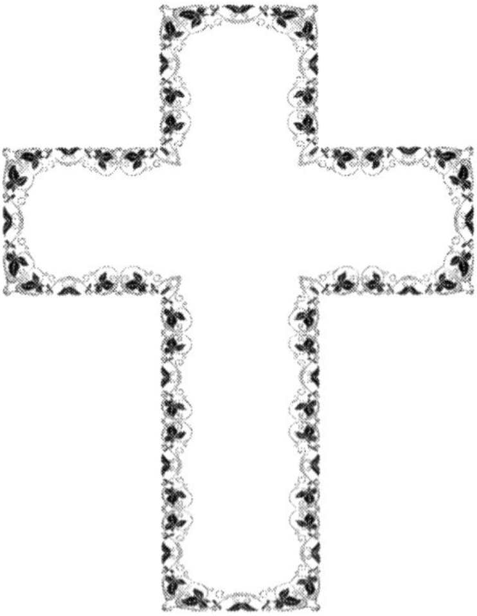

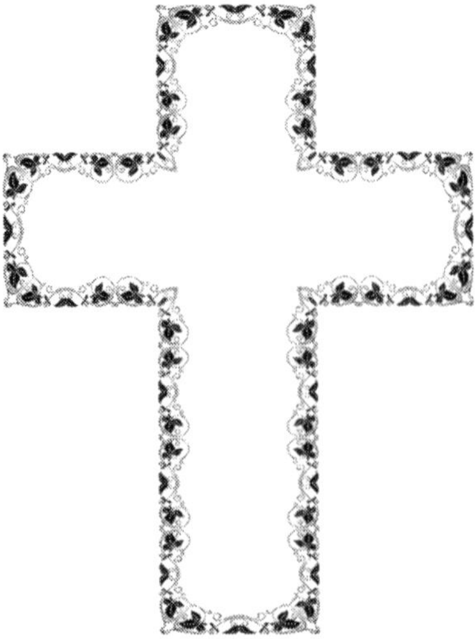

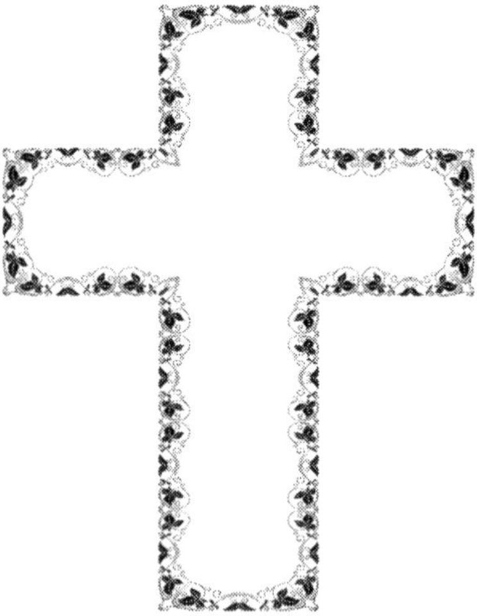

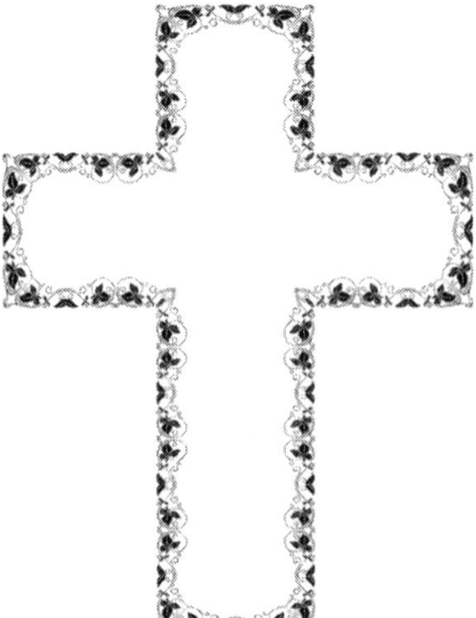

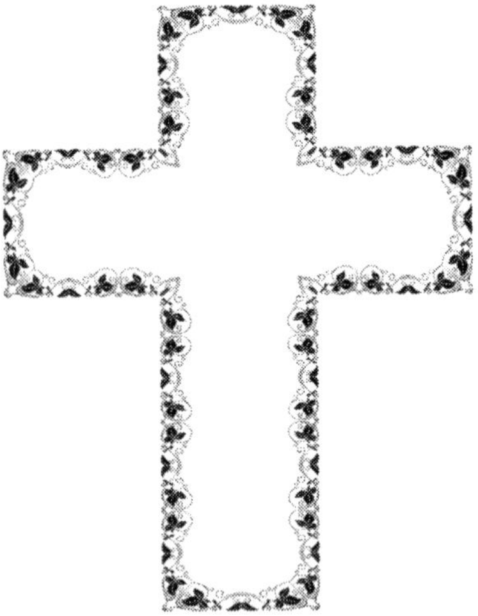

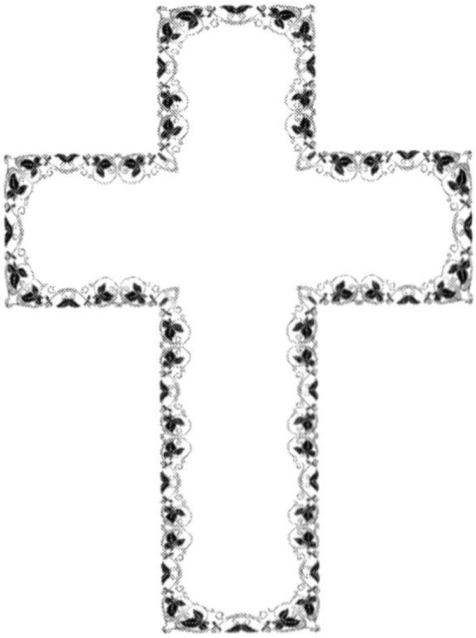

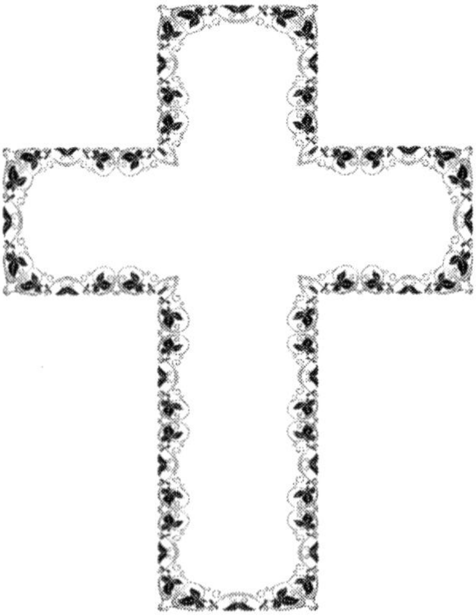

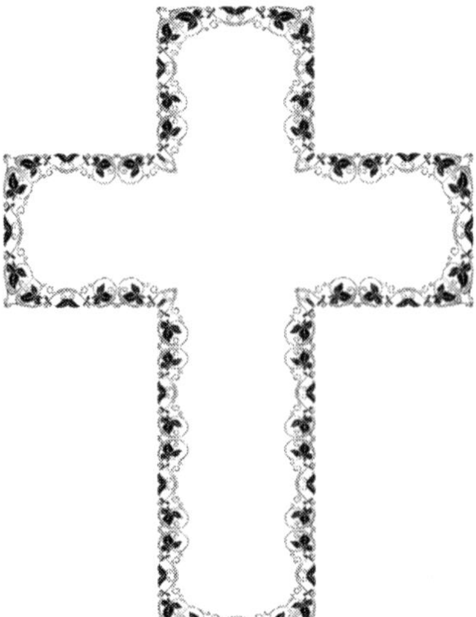

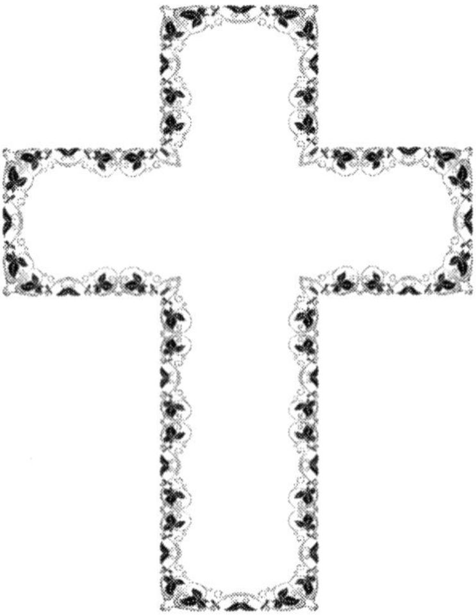

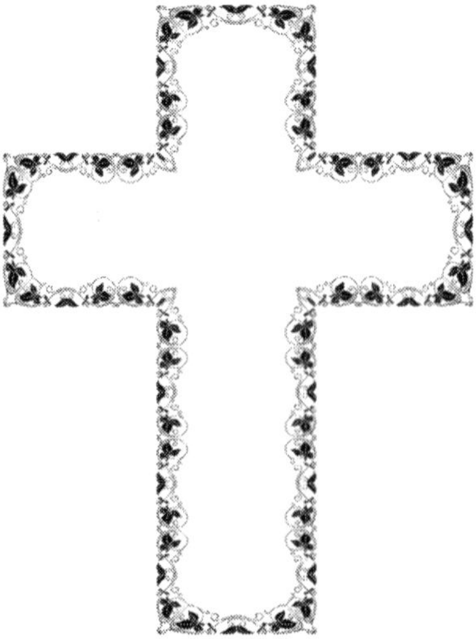

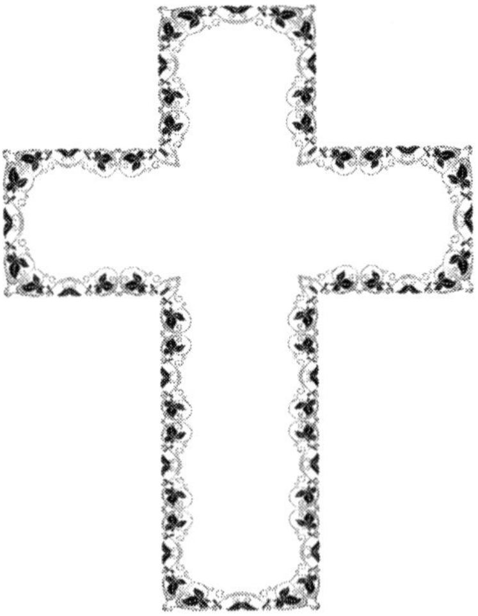

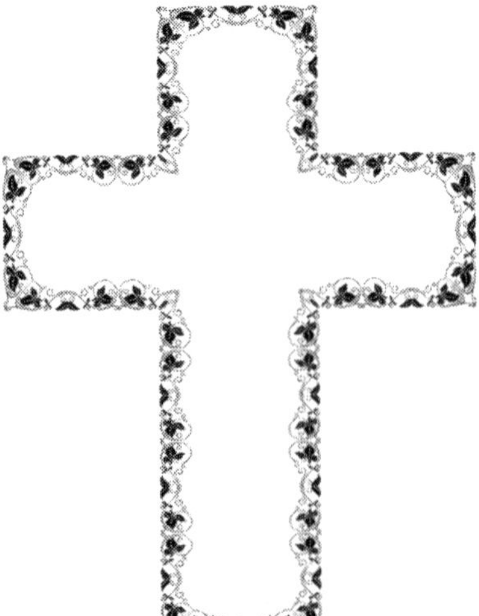

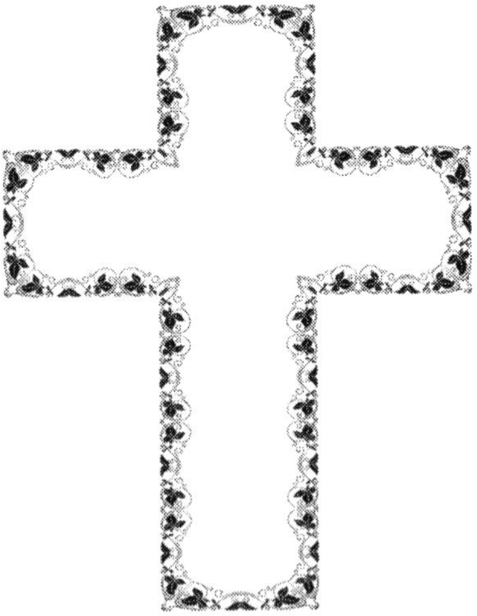

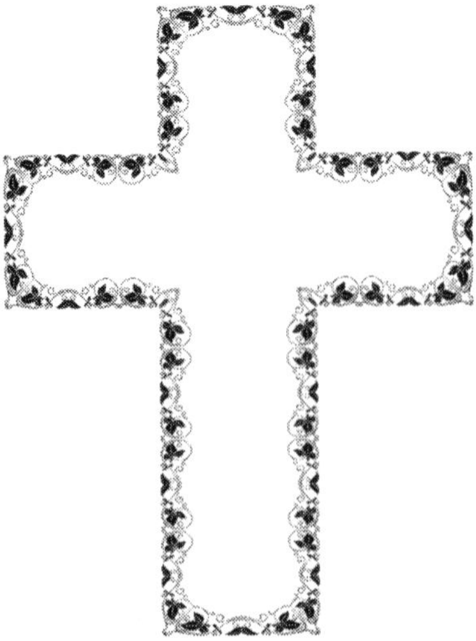

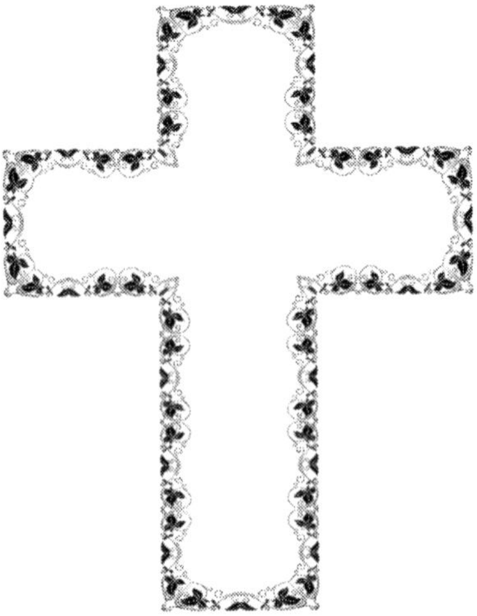

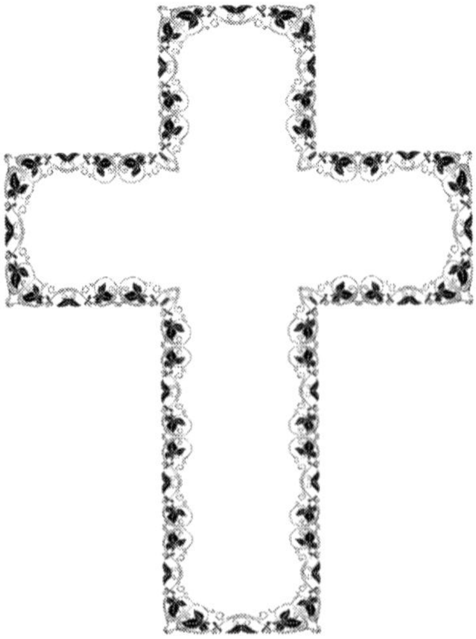

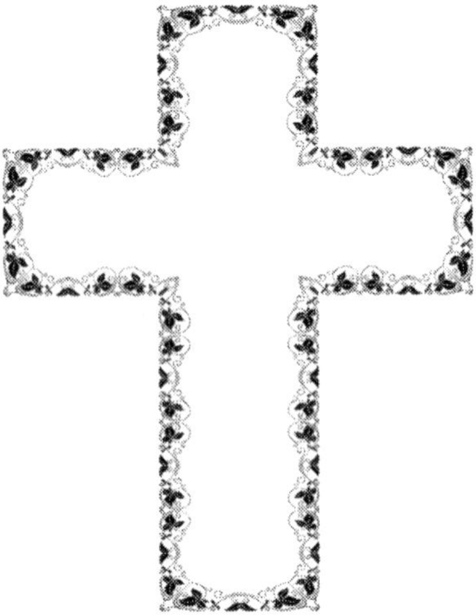

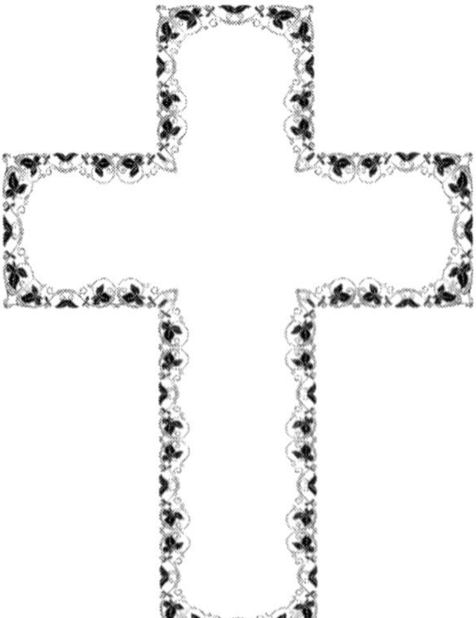

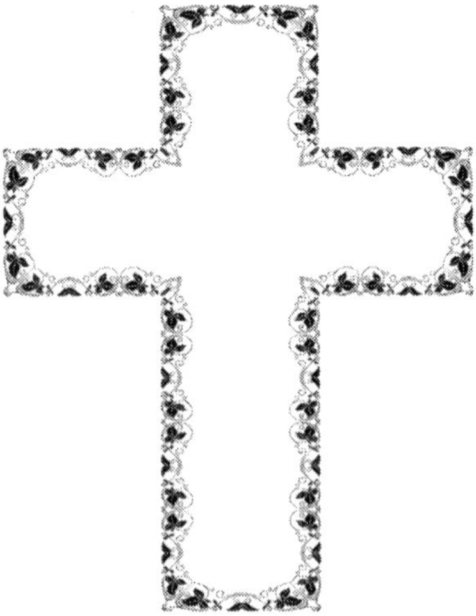

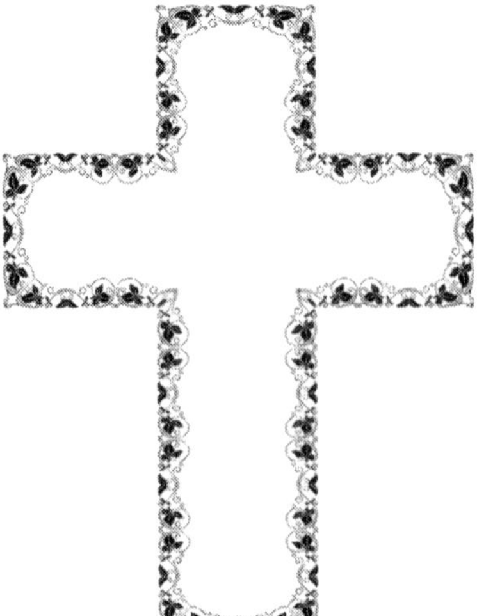

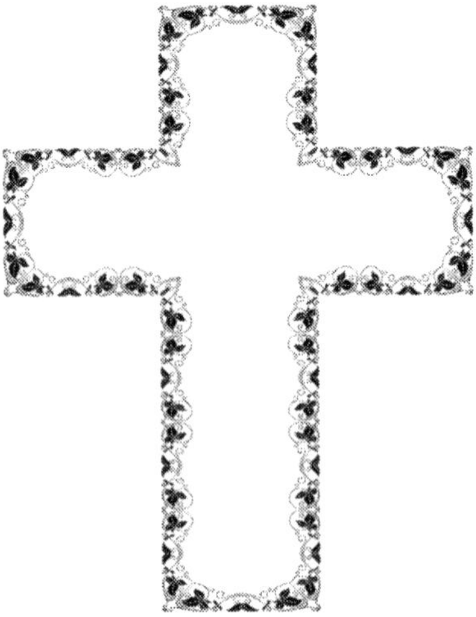

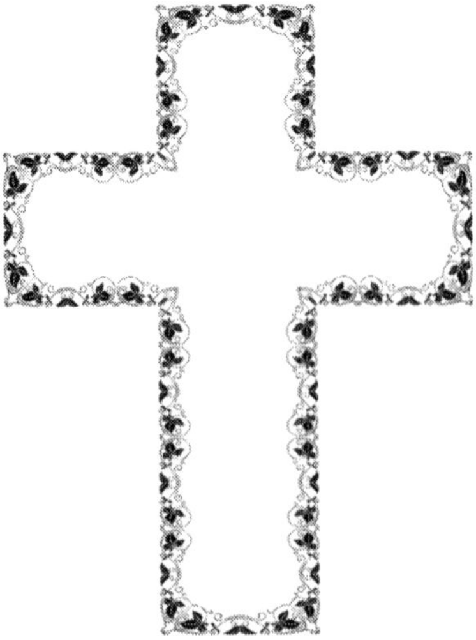

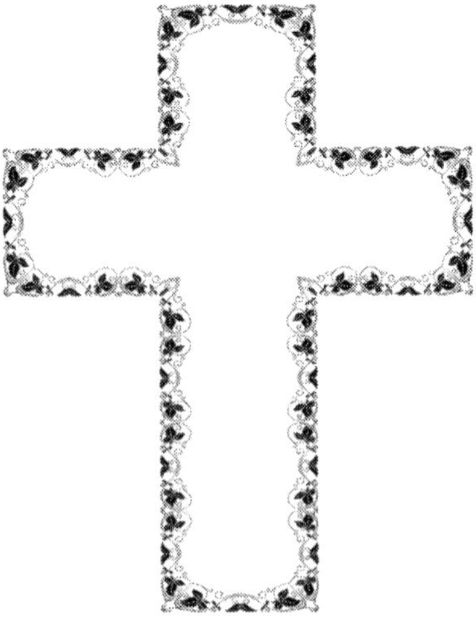

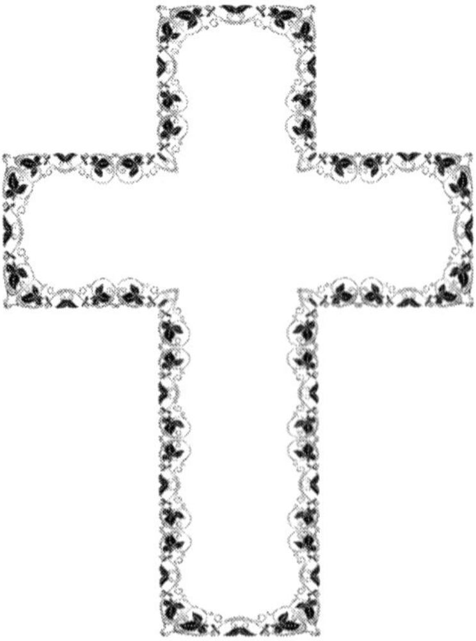

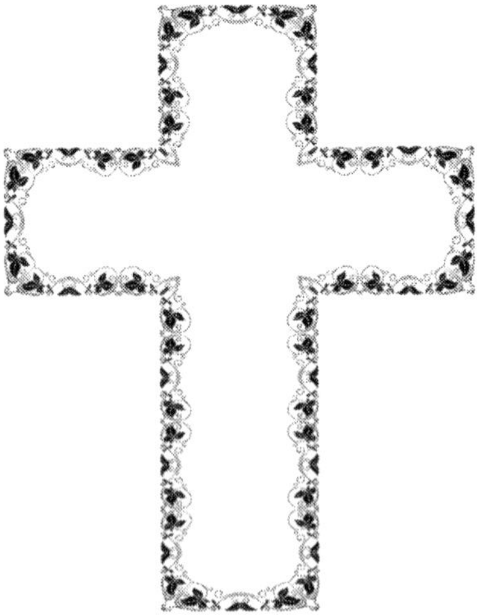

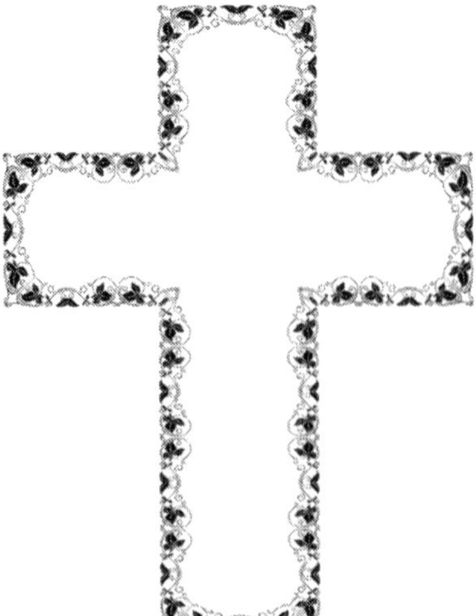

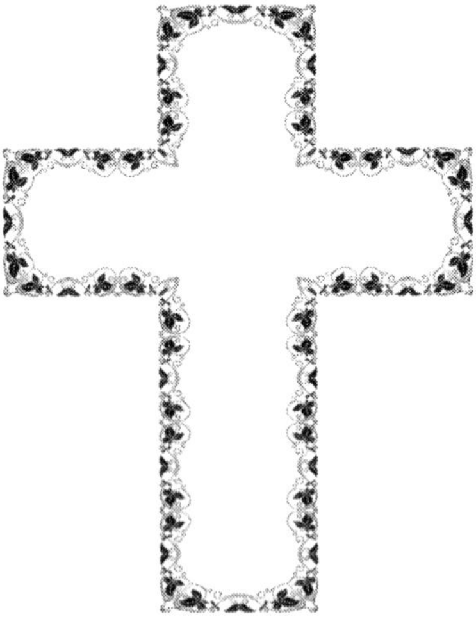

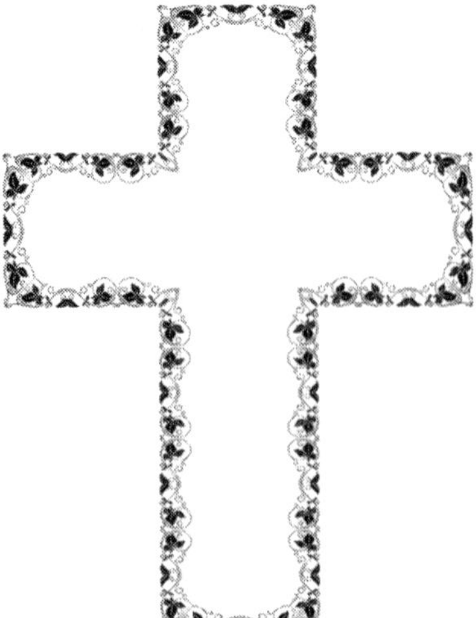

Made in the USA
Middletown, DE
09 May 2022

65559003R00057